ANIMALS AT RISK!

Caribou

by Rachel Grack

BELLWETHER MEDIA • MINNEAPOLIS, MN

Blastoff! Readers are carefully developed by literacy experts to build reading stamina and move students toward fluency by combining standards-based content with developmentally appropriate text.

Level 1 provides the most support through repetition of high-frequency words, light text, predictable sentence patterns, and strong visual support.

Level 2 offers early readers a bit more challenge through varied sentences, increased text load, and text-supportive special features.

Level 3 advances early-fluent readers toward fluency through increased text load, less reliance on photos, advancing concepts, longer sentences, and more complex special features.

★ **Blastoff! Universe**

Reading Level

Grade
K

Grades
1–3

Grade
4

This edition first published in 2024 by Bellwether Media, Inc.

No part of this publication may be reproduced in whole or in part without written permission of the publisher. For information regarding permission, write to Bellwether Media, Inc., Attention: Permissions Department, 6012 Blue Circle Drive, Minnetonka, MN 55343.

Library of Congress Cataloging-in-Publication Data

Names: Koestler-Grack, Rachel A., 1973- author.
Title: Caribou / Rachel Grack.
Description: Minneapolis, MN : Bellwether Media, 2024. | Series: Blastoff! Readers. Animals at risk | Includes bibliographical references and index. | Audience: Ages 5-8 | Audience: Grades 2-3 | Summary: "Relevant images match informative text in this introduction to why caribou are at risk. Intended for students in kindergarten through third grade"-- Provided by publisher.
Identifiers: LCCN 2023004260 (print) | LCCN 2023004261 (ebook) | ISBN 9798886874181 (library binding) | ISBN 9798886876062 (ebook)
Subjects: LCSH: Caribou--Juvenile literature. | Caribou--Conservation--Juvenile literature.
Classification: LCC QL737.U55 K636 2024 (print) | LCC QL737.U55 (ebook) | DDC 599.65/8--dc23/eng/20230130
LC record available at https://lccn.loc.gov/2023004260
LC ebook record available at https://lccn.loc.gov/2023004261

Editor: Kieran Downs   Designer: Brittany McIntosh

Printed in the United States of America, North Mankato, MN.

Table of Contents

Snow Deer

Caribou are large deer. They live in the northern parts of the world. There are many **subspecies**.

Their large **antlers** stand out in their cold, snowy **habitats**.

antlers

herd

Caribou need wide habitats. Large **herds** travel across the **tundra**.

But habitats are getting smaller. People are mostly to blame.

Caribou Range

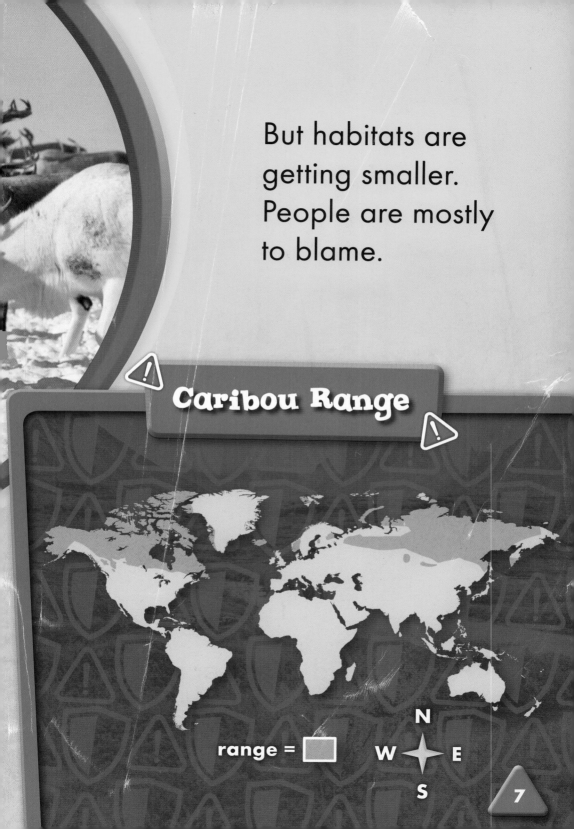

range = ▭

N
W — E
S

People build roads across caribou **migration** paths. They clear forests for logging and farmland.

Mining and oil drilling break up herds.

① people need oil

② people drill for oil on the tundra

③ caribou lose habitat

Climate change can cause warmer weather. This brings new animals north. More **predators** attack herds.

New animals also eat the same food as caribou. Caribou cannot find enough.

predator

Caribou Stats

Least Concern	Near Threatened	Vulnerable	Endangered	Critically Endangered	Extinct in the Wild	Extinct

conservation status: vulnerable

life span: up to 15 years

11

Save the Caribou!

Caribou keep their **ecosystems** healthy. They are food for other animals.

Their poop makes the soil healthy. It helps plants grow.

The World with Caribou

1

more caribou

2

more plants

3

healthy forests and grasslands

Wildlife workers **corral** caribou during birthing season.

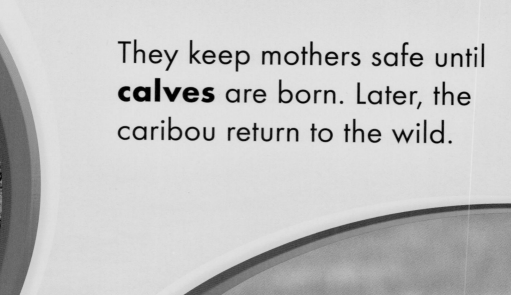

They keep mothers safe until **calves** are born. Later, the caribou return to the wild.

calf

Laws stop logging, mining, and oil drilling. In time, forests will regrow.

forest regrowth

Caribou may someday have larger habitats again.

Some governments set aside land for caribou. Herds can move freely.

Their numbers are slowly growing.
But many caribou still need help.

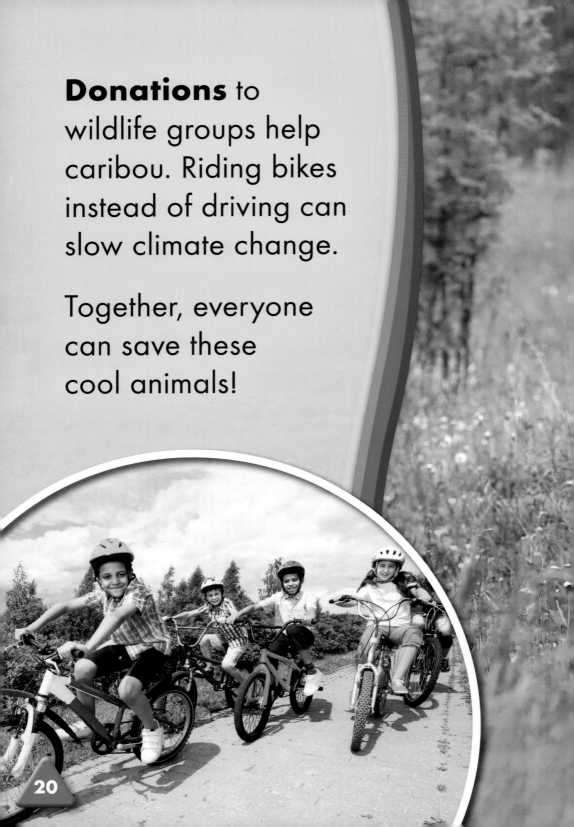

Donations to wildlife groups help caribou. Riding bikes instead of driving can slow climate change.

Together, everyone can save these cool animals!

Glossary

antlers—bony, branched horns on the heads of deer, moose, and caribou

calves—baby caribou

climate change—a human-caused change in Earth's weather due to warming temperatures

corral—to gather together in a pen

donations—gifts for a certain cause; most donations are money.

ecosystems—communities of plants and animals living in certain places

habitats—places and natural surroundings in which plants or animals live

herds—groups of caribou that live and travel together

laws—rules that must be followed

migration—the act of traveling from one place to another, often with the seasons

predators—animals that hunt other animals for food

subspecies—groups of one type of animal that live in different parts of the world

tundra—flat, treeless, frozen land found in far northern regions

To Learn More

AT THE LIBRARY

Emminizer, Theresa. *Roaming Caribou*. New York, N.Y.:
PowerKids Press, 2022.

Hansen, Grace. *Caribou Migration*. Minneapolis, Minn.:
Abdo Kids, 2021.

London, Martha. *Saving Caribou*. Lake Elmo, Minn.:
Focus Readers, 2021.

ON THE WEB

FACTSURFER

Factsurfer.com gives you
a safe, fun way to find
more information.

1. Go to www.factsurfer.com.

2. Enter "caribou" into the search box
   and click 🔍.

3. Select your book cover to see a list
   of related content.

Index

The images in this book are reproduced through the courtesy of: Sylvie Bouchard, front cover; BearFotos, p. 3; Mircea Costina, p. 4; Pim Leijen, p. 5; Sergey Krasnoshchokov, pp. 6, 12, 13 (top left), 18; Tonis Valing, p. 8; RachenStocker, p. 9 (top left); Vladimir Endovitskiy, p. 9 (top right); nenets, p. 9 (bottom); Holly Kuchera, p. 10; Ana Flasker, pp. 10-11; AlexDamansky, p. 13 (top right); Nataliya Hora, p. 13 (bottom); Alex Hsuan Tsui, p. 14; Jukka Jantunen, p. 15; YegoroV, p. 16; Kersti Lindstrom, p. 17; Ian William Hromada, p. 19; Sergey Novikov, p. 20; blickwinkel/ Alamy Stock Photo, pp. 20-21; FotoRequest, p. 23.